Injured
and
Scarred
but
Not Broken

SHARING QUESTIONS THAT LEAD TO MY WHOLENESS

WORKBOOK

QUEEN ESTHER LACEY

Author of
Sexually Driven & Sexually Driven II
Illustrations by Michaela Childs

authorHOUSE

AuthorHouse™
1663 Liberty Drive
Bloomington, IN 47403
www.authorhouse.com
Phone: 833-262-8899

Published by AuthorHouse   12/27/2021

ISBN: 978-1-6655-4691-1 (sc)
ISBN: 978-1-6655-4690-4 (e)

Contents

Introduction

There have been several reasons I have felt damaged or broken. In fact, trying to get this project publish caused me hurt. Mentally and emotionally scarred. I was trying to support the local small business, so I gave him money for publishing, and he took the money and ran. I wanted to get this project out to you, so I hired another publishing company. Meanwhile, I'll let the Lord and the courts avenge me for that situation.

Injury comes in different forms. The three forms I think about are **physical, mental, and emotional.** When I speak on injury, I speak on sickness, heartbreak, low self-esteem, etc. Any form of abuse that would cause a distraction to prevent one from not being able to operate at 100% capacity, or to be happy, healthy, and whole.

2019 was a year of great physical injury for me. I endured so much sickness I thought I was going to die. In June, I had brain surgery. There was a tumor pressing against my optical nerve, and it damaged my optical nerve so much that it is extremely hard to see out of my left eye. I was also told I still have a mass in that eye. While recovering from the brain surgery, I developed a blood clot in my lungs. Moreover, I was also diagnosed with diabetes, and my blood pressure was stroke level for so long it caused my heart to enlarge. On top of that, I also developed bronchitis. During this time, family members were also going through their own life battles of injuries – breast cancer, bone cancer, lung cancer, stroke, and drug addiction. November 23rd was the last announcement given to me – stage 3 chronic kidney disease. Back-to-back illnesses, I was wondering what is going on. Yes, 2019 was a horrible year as far as physical health goes. As I prayed, I realize there had been several events of injury in my life. Not even realizing the scares they have left.

Fast forward to 2020, the mass they saw, yes, it is a tumor behind my eye which pushes my eye out a little and it (the tumor) is sitting right on the optical nerve. Removing it may cause total blindness in my left eye. I have several tumors on my thyroids, and one sitting on my kidneys, which they feel may be the cause of my stroke level blood pressure.

Let us say I have spent a lot of time in the hospital.

This workbook outlines various events describing my personal experiences of injury (some leaving scares). I thought it was the end for me, but God!!! I may be injured and scared, but I am not broken. I walk in wholeness.

I consider this to be a workbook because I share my personal testimonies which I call Open Book

Moments and poems, then I provide you (the reader) space for your comments/notes. I believe this will give you a moment to reflect on your own lives.

I hope someone, anyone, is blessed by this workbook, even if it is just one.

BE ENCOURAGED EVERY DAY!!!

Queen Esther Lacey

Dedication

To all that have been a part of my growth and journey to love myself!

An Open Book Moment

Being Covered – There are dangers seen and unseen. I did not realize it at the time, but looking back on things, I see I brought a lot of things on myself. My self-esteem was so low; wherever I received attention, I soaked it all up. This explains the flirtation. Growing up the guys would call it teasing of the male genitals (putting it nicely).

Thinking back on one of my trips to Jamaica, I remember situations I put myself in. It was about seven of us making the trip. It was exciting and the island is so beautiful. We went out on the sunset boat ride. The boat had a bottom that you could see through. Some got out (with Suba gear on) and got closer looks. Not me, lol. We would be out on the water until the sun was setting. Guess that is why they called it sunset boat rides. It was priceless. Then there was another ride we went on and we sat on the shore side, and the locals would just step out in the water, grab a few lobsters, and cook them up. Or they would take us to the park and grill up a dish. Or we just walked the beach side and meet people selling items or partying; it was just so free. I understand why they always say, "No Problem."

So here comes the local cutie that gives me a little attention. I knew he was young, but they said age is just a number. He was driving the jet ski and asked if I wanted a ride. Now you know, I was too scared. Each day he would find me and ask to take me out. Yes, he wore me down. Got me on that jet ski and took me out into the deep. Now I am under this young boy's subjection. He showed me beautiful parts of the island, then pulled into this cave. He pulled over and stopped the jet ski and got off. He told me to get off and proceeded to make sexual advances. He wanted to have sex right there in the cave. I do not know if this was a part of the sightseeing, but I did not want to view that part of the island. Why did I put myself in this position again? Referring to many years prior being raped at gun point. Am I that desperate to be wanted that I give the wrong message to men that are not going to treat me right? I finally got the message to him that I did not want to get involved like that. We got back on the jet ski and came on back to the hotel.

The next day the girls and I were scheduled to go on a different type of boat ride. As we were walking towards the boat another cutie that I was receiving attention from caught up with me. He was walking with me towards the boat, and he put his hand in the back pocket of my jeans. We were just walking and laughing and suddenly I hear someone yelling out "Take your hand out her pocket!" It was the guy from the jet ski. I did not understand what was going on. Apparently when a guy puts his hand in the pocket, it means that is his girl. We reached the boat and the girls, and I got on. Suddenly there was this big water wave that came over us on the boat. The guys on the boat that was taking us out on the tour started cussing and saying what is wrong with that guy. The jet ski guy had turned the jet ski in a way that it kicked up a wave of water over the boat. I said, "Sorry guys, I think that might be my fault."

Later that evening we went out to one of the local bars/grills, and there were some guys there who said to me "We know you." I responded, "You do not know me; I am not from around here." They said, "We saw you on the beach with the white jeans on." I realized this was a small island because it was me. Remember me with the hand in the pocket? Yes, white jeans! Causing problems.

Then there was the cook at the hotel, yes, he was a tall cutie, and I flirted with him and met him on the roof top. Just to talk, lol. He gave me his number and wanted us to visit each other. Our conversing was becoming increasingly intimate. However, I met up with one of the guys from the boat ride, and the cook saw it and was upset. My friends told me that I hurt him, and he was upset. I wondered what would have happened had I just talked to him. Well, I will never know.

Oh my gosh, have I come out to the island and created a mess with the men? I thank God for covering me, but I realize I had an issue of wanting to be loved. I just go about it all wrong.

What drives you?

Do you ever find yourself seeking attention?
Do you seek validation? Where do you think
that comes from? What is the root?

Comments / Notes

An Open Book Moment

That is Not Love – Sitting in the private room in the emergency department of the hospital. I do not even remember how I got there. The nurse was examining me and asking several questions. I answered them all, but to tell you the truth I was not extremely focused. What was I doing there? The nurse walked out for a minute, and when she returned, she handed me a pamphlet. It spoke to the nature of being a battered woman or in an abusive relationship. Something to that fact. Okay, why was she giving this to me? I am not battered, and I am not in an abusive relationship

I love my man and he love me!!!

My man loves me so much he wants to keep me all to himself. I do not go around my family that much because they do not really understand him. When I get off work, I come straight home. I do not have a car, so I take the bus. He knows the exact time I should be home. If I get home too early or too late that means I must have been fooling around with some man. Anything outside of doing what is normal for me, upsets him, and that would deserve punishment. Hey, even in the bible it says God chastens them who He loves. That proves even the more how much my man loves me because he is always beating me for something. I would just have to try harder to not upset him.

I know when to have his dinner cooked and served to him. When he was done, I would clear the table. I had to have the dishes cleaned by the required time, and do not think about having a snack later, that was out of the question.

When it was time to get ready for bed, I would take my shower or bath. I also knew just how long to spend in the bathroom. When I came to the bedroom if I was not clean enough, I had to get things right. That is how much he loved me, he wanted me clean

There were many times he had to punish me because I was always messing up. One time he cut me on the face because he said it was a sign to the world that I was a whore. I had a sexual addiction, and he was trying to make me a better person. He would tell me that people would tell him they saw me with this and that person. I just embarrassed him in the neighborhood. I was not with other people, but he did not believe me a lot of times. He would drag me to this and that man and say to them, "Now tell me again what you said about her." Many times, they would not repeat it, but he would have already punished me for it.

So, this day he had just enough. He beat me so badly I guess I must have blacked out, and when I came to, I was in the private room in the emergency department. For some reason, people want to take away the only man that ever loved me. They say that is not love!

What do you know about abuse?

What is abuse? What does it look like? Would you know if you were being abused? Name a few types of abuse.

Comments / Notes

What do you know about addiction?

What is addiction? Would you know
if you had an addiction? What does it
look like? Name a few addictions.

Comments / Notes

The Word states "it's not good for man to be alone"
I confessed I do not need a man; I can do everything on my own

I was claiming a life of celibacy
Because I was not allowing a man to touch me

Because of my past no man was ever going to hurt me again
No more being that receiving vessel for him to release in

Men have taught me sex is all that I am good for,
So now my life was worthless since I closed that door

I began to develop a hate for men
Truth be told, I hated myself and many times wanted my life to end

Somewhere in the mist of it all, I was told self-pleasure is a healthy thing to do
When your flesh arises just do you

Nobody would know I was quenching my fleshly thirst
Things should be better right, no it got worst

My fleshly cravings just grew more and more
It was not even a self-gratification as it was before

I was preforming this act night and day
It had nothing to do with pleasure; for it had become a slave

This was not of God this was not in His plan

He designed sex to be a healthy exchange within the intimacy of a woman and man

I cannot talk to anyone about this strong hold that I am tied up and tangled in

I cannot tell anyone, not even my best friend

But thank God for today He sent my help

An obedient vessel that was not afraid to say that one word

(masturbation) it is wrong to please yourself

Today this struggle comes to its end

I shall no longer be tormented and bound for committing this sexual sin

An Open Book Moment

There is a chapter in the bible that tells a story about a woman that Jesus met at a well.

St. John 4:4-29 (I encourage you to read the whole chapter).

The first story in the bible that I read and related to, was this one. I always said, "If I were a woman in the bible, I would be this woman at the well." Then I would be a part of the #1 bestselling books of the bad girls of the bible.

Why do I feel that way? I have been married more than once, and I lived with a few men. But I love the part how the scripture shows Jesus met her where she was (in her sin) and came into her life where she wanted to share with everyone about the man she just met.

I was in a relationship with someone and I did not even know anything about him. I met him as a pen pal. I had no interest of being with anyone romantically. I had experience being raped at gun point, and that just damaged any thought to give myself to anyone. This was a perfect arrangement. He was in jail, and he could not express himself to me in a physical matter. The pen pal relationship went on for a few months, then he said he loved me and wanted us to take our relationship to the next level. I know he was not talking about marriage! How is that possible? My mother asked me not to move forward in that choice. I just figured she was speaking from a place of control, not from a place of love and warning. Hold that thought from earlier that I shared with you about being raped.

Time went on. I was really thinking about it and my friend was going to come with me to be a witness if I decided to go through with it. I also met one of his relatives, and she was willing to drive out of state if I would do it. In my mind it was like he was a free man, and this was normal. I imagined how the big day would be. We would say our "I dos," then I would go home with his relative, and he would go to his cell. There was nothing normal about that. One day his relative and I began to share, she said "You are really special if you are willing to take your relationship to that total commitment level with a man that committed that kind of crime." I said, "Well I will stick by him it was just robbery." She said, "No he is in there for rape and sodomizing an older lady." I did not know what sodomizing was, but I knew what rape was.

Remember that thought I told you to hang onto. I was raped and found out the man I was involved with was in jail for raping someone. I felt sick to my stomach and understood at that point why he never wanted me to come to court. The painful reality was he never loved me. If you get married, the jail system allows you to have weekend visits with your spouse. I guess the system was set up to keep families together. To me, it destroyed me to the point it was a thin line that landed me in my old room on the mental ward at the hospital. Once released from the hospital I was able to dissolve my relationship completely with someone that could lie and misrepresented himself on such a horrible level. If I could give a warning to women, to build their self-esteem up and do not settle. Do not get me wrong, there are good guys that just get caught up in the system. But there are the others!

A few years went by, and I got in another relationship with someone else. I met him on the outside, but he ended up going on the inside (jail). This was one of the good ones I spoke about, but he got caught up in the drug world. Once he got the right help, he became an incredibly good man, but he was not mine any more by this time. Some other woman took him right away from me. If I wanted to be with him, I would have to become the other woman. Wow, he was mine and now he belonged to another.

That led to being with so many others, and when the Lord met me at my well, I was willing to give it all up. Is there a husband in my future? I do not know, but I will make sure I am prayed up, so that I will be able to discern if HE IS THE ONE!

Do you think you are valuable?

Have you ever settled just to be loved? Do
you even really know what love is? Is your
need to not be alone overriding your ability to
recognize a wolf that is in sheep clothing?

Comments / Notes

An Open Book Moment

When two are getting married usually the man is to love his wife, and the wife is to respect her husband. The true reason I may be all alone is because I do not have any love, and I give no respect to marriage.

All the little sad puppies come to me the same way. Telling me how things at home aren't this way and that way. I would ask have they tried praying, but then my self-esteem would be so low that they would wear me down. I loved receiving flowers at work. They would be so beautiful, and it would give me attention, but I could not say who they were from. One would get the rent paid; one would make sure there were Christmas gifts for the children. However, the way I would give of myself was so degrading.

I would start to believe they cared. Once I believed that, it was like I would turn into another person. I would be everything they told me they did not receive at home. I totally blocked out that they had a home to go to. From fixing a plate of food to becoming the food on the plate and serving myself. I told one guy I was his and only his, and I wrapped myself in ribbons and a big bow and told him he had to open his gift with tongue only. One guy I would meet out on the road, and between the car seats I would display my acrobatic skills.

I would come home and be confronted by wives; I started to believe my own lies. No, I am not involved with your husband, as I would be on my way to church. I started to believe I was an agent of the devil to take down every man. I was starting to hate men. Just thinking about them releasing on or in me disgusted me. There was one that even brought in women to my bed. One guy loved to have his dinner ready and served as soon as he came over. He then demanded his body rubbed down and his feet rubbed, then satisfy his manhood. When that was a wrap, he would turn over and take a nap. Many times, he would get a call and must leave. That used to hurt because no matter what he said about the one that was not taking care of him, when she called, it was bye to me.

Respect, what is that? Before I can give it to others, I must receive it for myself.

I have made the choice that I WILL NOT serve another man sexually that is not my husband. There is more to me than what I behold between my legs. If your household is messed up, I will pray for you for real, and that is all I got. I have been so broke that I could make one call and money would not be a problem. Instead, I chose to send up prayers. I wanted to be clean, I want to be respected. I wanted to be received as a virtuous woman. I do not want any woman to feel uncomfortable when I am around their husband. I am incredibly careful how I carry myself now.

My last prayer regarding being with a man is if it is His will for me to be a wife, clean me up!!! I want to be submissive and not lustfully seductive. To be honorable and not to be a whore. To be respectful and not ratchet. For my husband to not have any fear nor any doubt.

Respecting Myself and Marriage

Young man what does marriage mean to you
When under so many beds you leave your shoes

You say you love me; how can you release that from your mouth
When you were just receiving the love juices from another's love spout

I would be setting myself up for failure right from the start
For it is not love you carry for me, that is lust in your heart

Being single does not mean I am desperate so I should settle for you
For me being the rib there is special side I belong to

Being single means, I am spending time with my Lord and being bathe in precious oils
I shall not allow your smooth words to trick me into letting my goods spoil

If you will lie down on her with me, then you will lie down with another on me
Being single I do not have to worry about that hurt, and I remain disease free

I know my value and I know my worth
I am sure creating someone for me is a small thing compared to creating the whole earth

An Open Book Moment

Denial – Over and over again I would tell myself 'I am not a hoe, nor am I a whore, nor am I a prostitute, nor am I a loose woman. I am a woman that just wants to be loved.' However, it appeared I was living that type of lifestyle. That is how you are viewed anytime you sleep with several men no matter how innocent you think you are. Each one I would treat like they were the only one in my life, and the things I would do with them I would tell them I have never done it before. I just actually learn the pattern of a man, and I played on it. I could be wrong, but my theory was men were very sexual. I would tell them I would pleasure them, and they would do anything. Some I did not sleep with, just the promise of it got them to do things.

Having one guy drive me to another guy not knowing what they were doing. Having one or two or more guys send me flowers to work. I was such an actress when I received the flowers at work. I thirsted for that attention to appear that I was receiving love.

Sometimes they were married, so the fact that they could not be around, I would tell myself that was good. They would tell me all the problems they had at home. I believed they loved me, and I would not give them any trouble. I would just perform on demand.

When I would attend church, I would feel so messed up. Not because I let God down, but it would be then that I felt dirty. I would see other women singing on the praise and worship team or the choir, and they looked so holy to me. They looked pure and clean and so Godly. That is what would jack me up. I would wish I were a virgin again. Then I have a drink or get high and start the game all over again. I have heard the best relationships are those that you are friends first. That is so foreign to me. Could I be friends with a man? I have no clue how to be a man's friend. I mean I might start conversing with him on general stuff, but then all I knew how to do is take the topic to sex. I am so self-aware of it now that I am extra careful talking to people's husbands (or any male for that matter) because I am trying hard to be a good girl now. I am trying to believe I have more to offer than what is between my legs, and I get so incredibly angry when someone insinuate towards sex. It is a fight! It is a battle! I am even attacked in my sleep. I genuinely want complete deliverance from this.

You see her smiling all the time, but the truth is every day she is
tormented of her past and feels dirty and ugly because of it

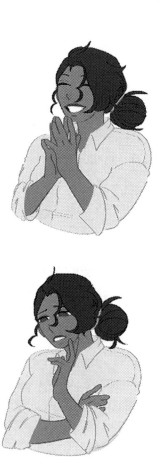

Do you realize denial delays deliverance?

Is there anything that your heart knows, and you hold it in thinking you are protecting yourself? Most of the time what we really end up doing is not protecting but hurting. The first thing we need to do is come out of denial and release.

If there is something that you have kept in thinking you are protecting but it is destroying you, write it down. You do not have to share it if you desire not to. The point is just to release it.

Comments / Notes

What are your motives?

Have you ever been there for others and do not receive that same level of support back to you? What drives you to be there for others? Why do you look for them to be there for you? Do you not believe God will have a ram in the bush for you?

Comments / Notes

An Open Book Moment

Balance - This weekend has really been rough. The job has taken me to a level of stress like never before. I want to quit so badly. The car needs an oil change, and I have $1.67 in my checking account and .20 cents in my savings. Trying to get my taxes filed so that I can go grocery shopping. I looked at my spending and my giving, and it just does not balance.

All someone must do is say they need, and I give. I have given my all. I need to get my house right first. I believe there is scripture that reflects on having your house in order first.

Why do I always feel like others matter more than me? My plans – get rid of the entire credit card debit, get a nice apartment that I will love to live in and get my health under control. Not necessarily in that order.

Right now, if I cannot help anyone, I must trust they will be all right. I cannot save the world!

An Open Book Moment

As young as 9 I remember going to group therapy, so I knew very well what that was about. As an adult, it continued but I learned after being put in the mental hospital you cannot express that you want to kill yourself, or you do not want to live because that can get you the residency of bare walls and 24-hour watch to make sure that does not happen. Yes, a few times I was checked into the mental ward. Looking back and understanding mental illness, I do not know if I so much wanted to die. I just wanted my world to have a better view. I wanted some sunshine, and it was always raining.

It was an endless cycle because I learned what to say, and I was in control of how far we would take it. Somethings I had locked up and threw away the key. Sessions would be of no avail because I would simply stop going. Or if I felt I could manage things because the meds were working, I would determine that to be a suitable time to stop taking them. Of course, that would start the entire process over again. Checking in and sharing what I want to release then checking out.

This has been my pattern all my life.

I felt so alone out here in AZ. I felt guilty that I was not in NY tending to the needs of my mother and my family. I felt trapped!!! I was spending money on things and then giving the items away. You learn people will tolerate you because there are items they know they will be blessed with if they just stick around.

You see the adult that has it all together, but the truth is, she walks in the hurt from her childhood

What does to have a sound mind mean to you?

Do you know what mental illness is? If you were mentally ill, would you seek help? Do you think it makes a person not a part of a normal society?

Comments / Notes

An Open Book Moment

Replacing one with the other – I thought about how my life was going and I realized something is still missing. I have a decent job, the love of family, NEVER had so many friends in my life. I was still missing stability in my life. I was still moving from apartment to apartment and changing my membership with churches like you chose a different vacation location every year for your summer pleasure.

I was so focused on the fact that I was not sleeping around, and I was living celibate that I did not realize I replaced that with something else. Purse shopping! I mean do not get it twisted, I love a nice purse, but it was like a drug to me. I would spend thousands in one shot. It was like I could go into a MK store or a Coach store and would not leave out without three to five bags. If someone was with me, yes, they would have to get one too. It was like I would see the bag and my mind completely would be lost. Then if I pick up two or three bags, the salesperson will zoom in and offer to start a hold for me. That is when the foreplay began. It was like I had a new friend, and I was getting attention. We would laugh and they would seem so interested. We were using each other. They get the commission, and I was having a void filled. Then I get up to the register and the next partner in this ménage trio would say one thousand and whatever. As they swiped my card or took my cash I would climax. Then they would hand me my bags and act like we did not just have something between us, and they would beckon for the next. I would then feel like a nobody again so as I exit the store, I would begin to think I will just give them away.

I have realized this is not normal, and a cry for returning to my first love spiritually and to my therapist and meds naturally. I realized I still have some healing to do. I still have some things going on chemically that only meds and God can alter.

I know who and whose I am, I just realize that I am not yet enjoying life to the fullest. Someone sent me an encouraging word from the Lord and referred to the scripture Jeramiah 29:11. I want to live in the plans God has planned for me!

Not replacing one for the other!

How confident are you in knowing oneself?

Would you know if you had an addiction? Is there anything that has a strong call that you must answer? List the things that you cannot do without, and exam why you feel this way.

Comments / Notes

An Open Book Moment

Yesterday's pain is a set up for today's purpose - Last night my thoughts went back to a time when I was in a relationship with someone that took me down a dark road. This person was not someone that I would have pictured to hook up with, but I did. Once in it, it seemed like the only way to get out of it was going to be through death, but to God be the glory. I remember one of the days starting off going to a food shelter in Yonkers, NY. We had been drinking and I needed to use the rest room. I did not know what kind of place it was; I just had to go to the bathroom. Once I came out the bathroom my partner was sitting at the table eating and told me to sit down and eat too. I was so nervous. I said we cannot do this. He said eat.

Then we proceeded to make our way to Manhattan (the city). Once arriving there he took me to some back alley, and he obtained a drug for us to consume. I did not know what it was, but because I did whatever he told me to do I took it as well. To know what it was, it was angel dust. My understanding angel dust is laced with either animal tranquilizer or embalming fluid. We walked the streets and there must have been a time we blacked out because when I came to myself, I was pinned up on this fence, and my partner was laid out on the sidewalk.

I remembered looking up and across the street was a church. I had to go to the restroom, and we proceeded to go into the church hoping to use the bathroom. They did not want to let us in. Thinking back, wow, all I could think I must have been really dirty that a church did not want to let me in. They finally let us in.

Once I came out the bathroom, he said, "Let us sit and see what is going on." We sat in the back of the church high and dirty. That is the way I felt. But no one said anything to us. No one ever came to us.

I am not sure why God allowed that memory to come back now, but the Saturday morning the 24th of September in the year 2016, I went to a prayer breakfast and the speaker spoke about taking the mask off. She brought out how God called us to different things, but we hide behind the mask. I found myself so much in her message I had to come out of denial. Then afterwards they were allowing the ladies to take the mask home. The masked I received did not have strings on it and I took that as a sign that I am never to wear a mask again. I must get over the fear of rejection and low self-esteem and doing God knows what just to be accepted.

Then that evening the ladies went out to a restaurant. It was just for ladies. Classy ladies 'n' what not was the theme. We were to wear a black dress and red lipstick. Just an evening where it was not your birthday or anything, just a time to celebrate being a lady and feeling sexy.

Well, the teaching I received from the church growing up you did not wear make-up, and if you did you defiantly did not wear red. That meant the Jezebel spirit. You know people really need to study that spirit, because more people carry it, and they do not have on red lipstick. Anyway, you would not believe how hard it was for me to put it on, but I did. It is funny how you will hold onto your childhood teachings (right or wrong). When I put that red lipstick on, I felt like I could do anything. I could be any type of woman that the situation called for. It was power in the red.

I have lived a life putting myself down and never thinking I was good enough. That night's experience of my black dress and red lipstick was a rebirthing of being a beautiful woman. It was like an ugly duckling turned into a beautiful swan. It might have been a meaningless thing to someone else, but it felt so good to me. It did not even matter if I was beautiful to the next person, I just felt alive. I always felt I was not wanted but not this night. Those thoughts were not riding my brain waves.

Prayer

I pray that God will always allow me to see me as He sees me. That He will give me the heart and compassion and discernment to see others in their need and/or hurt. If I attend a church, I will not be blind to the ones that He leads to the church. I do not care how they look, and/or smell. I will look pass the outward and see them through spiritual eyes.

An Open Book Moment

Is it just me – What I am about to express is not just limited to one type of person. Anyone lonely or with low self-esteem can fall victim. So, I am on the cell phone conversing with a male, it is basic stuff. Then he asked me for a picture, so I sent a couple pictures that were already seen by the public on my social media page. To my surprise, later that evening I received a text from him. He requested another picture that was more revealing. He was asking for a picture of yours truly in my birthday suit, and I am not talking about the outfit I wore on my birthday, lol. I responded to the "minister" that I felt that was distasteful. He apologized and that was the end of that.

I get this more than I care to. Yes, I want to be admired and I want someone interested, but is that all they are interested in, and it is always the first thing? So of course, it is me because if that is how I am approached from more than one guy, then I am thinking I am the common denominator. I am thinking it is the way I say things, or when in person, it is my body language. Should I just give up on this fantasy of being in love and just give into the demand of the hour?

I know it is said men are visual, but does that mean when we are conversing, he has already undressed me and had his way with me? Is it me that needs to be more open minded to the subject? Am I so damaged that I will never receive love because I go overboard with my thoughts on not defiling my temple?

Do you think you are worthy?

Do you ever feel like you are only good for one thing? Sex! Do you think that is a norm? Do you think just because you spend time with a man or if he buys you dinner that is the price you must pay?

Comments / Notes

Do you know that life and death are in the power of the tongue?

What things are you saying about yourself? What comes easy for you to say? Write down five things about yourself.

Comments / Notes

Do you know what you think about yourself will determine who you are?

Now if any of the five things you wrote down about yourself are negative, turn that around and write down five (or more) good things. This may take a little longer. From this point on when you are speaking about yourself, think of something positive to say. Even if you must give it an extra minute.

Comments / Notes

That Hidden Sin

Lord, please forgive me for the hidden sin
The one that seems to have a stronghold to keep me from making it in

The one that keeps me from worshiping in spirit and in truth
The one You have spoken in Your Word to be an abomination to You

I do not act on it because I know that it is not right
But the desire is there, and I am afraid I might
give up, give in, and lose the fight

I cannot tell others about this because they would not understand
How can I confession salvation when I would
rather be with her than with a man

What made me like this Lord, what went wrong, why am I this way
Do I just live my life with
this inner turmoil &
struggle, or do I continue to fast and pray

I feel like I am the only one, but I know there are others
Maybe I experience this to help another sister or brother

Was I born this way or when I was molested
as a child, it was imparted into me
Will this be my thorn in the flesh or will I one day be set free

Is it a need to just get rid of lust or is it deeper than that
Being in my mind headed to my heart and
then the only thing left is the very act

Lord, please help me; free me from this hidden sin
I do not want to be lost to hell's fire when here on earth my life comes to an end.

How do you identify yourself?

Have you ever wanted to or have experience a
same sex partner relationship? If you have, did
you go back to the opposite sex partner? Do
you think you were born this way, or was it
introduce or forced on you making you that way?

Comments / Notes

An Open Book Moment

It only takes one time – POW, BANG! Your first thought may be that I was trying to describe a scene from Batman when he is fighting the bad guys. Pow, Bang!! Across the screen would be a fist connecting with a jaw, and in bold colors would be the words POW and BANG.

Well, this is no scene from Batman or any other superhero cartoon, but this is real life.

He was just the type women say they want. Tall dark and handsome! He was attentive and took care of my every need. I wanted for nothing. He was the type to take his time and make sure I was comfortable and at ease with any new adventure he put before me. He was very playful when the time called for it and sensitive at other times. We could go out and paint the town red, or we could watch a movie at home in our pj's, or we could just sit and talk, while he painted my toenails. He was amazing.

Things started to change. He started hanging out all the time without me. One night a friend of mine asked me if I wanted to go out. I said to myself why should I stay home? So, I told my friend I would go out with her.

When I returned home, he had arrived before me. I came into the bedroom and was standing by the closet, and he began to question me as to where I had been for the evening. I responded with since he went out, I did not want to be alone and my friend called me to go out, so I did.

Without warning – POW, his fist connected with my face.

BANG, my head went into the closet door. I was in such shock I froze. That only allowed his fist to connect with my face again. Again, my head went into the closet door. I began to cry and inquire why. He accused me of cheating. Must have been his guilt because I never stepped out on him. Why wasn't I allowed to go out with my friends and enjoy myself as he was allowed?

After things settled down, he said he was sorry, and he did not know what came over him. I said to him it seemed like he enjoyed it. His response was, "Yes," he did a little. That was the first time he hit me, and that is all it takes is one time.

What does true forgiveness of others mean to you?

You say you forgive, but every time that name comes up you keep telling the same story. You have not truly forgiven.

Write down the name of the person that when you think of them you attach negativity to them.

Keep praying for God to take the hate out of your heart. Each day focus on releasing this from your heart.

When that name can be mentioned and your mind does not send you straight to the negative, then you know you have truly forgiven.

Comments / Notes

What does true forgiveness of oneself mean to you?

What if the one you need to forgive is self?
It is said in cases where women have been
raped, they blame themselves. They are not
at fault, but it is so hard to not blame self.

Comments / Notes

Do you know you are wonderfully made?

Make yourself a list of positive things to say about yourself each day. Affirmations, if you will. Whether it is a scripture and/or a saying you heard.

Comments / Notes

When I awaken this morning, I knew things for me had changed
My spirit was so much lighter, I was no longer the same

I had truly given up a battle that was never mine
I truly was able to forgive for things that happen to me before the age of nine

I was like clay on the potter's wheel without any shape or form
You took the innocent from my body which caused a lifetime of harm

I hated myself and others around me
I spent a lifetime making bad choices of which I could not be set free

It was embedded in me so deeply that my only purpose was to serve from laying on my back
That I even took on the guilt of it being my fault when at gun point, I was attack

I would curse the day the vessel of my mother gave birth
There were so many times I wanted and tried to end my life here on earth

But I found out all my pain and hurt was kept alive and kept
feeding off the fact that I could not forgive
I would have to let go and trust God to be free and in abundance to live

So, I decided to forgive you from all you have done to me
I shall walk in the victory of no condemnation, yes truly made free

YES, I FORGIVE you and I shall walk in purpose, not defeat
The rivers of water that flow through my belly shall no longer be bitter, it shall be sweet

Last night I could hardly sleep
I finally recognized and receive the key to be free

I have been taught through ugly experiences as a child that I was only good for one thing
When asked, my response was nothing to the table, I bring

I devalued myself and my worth
I was not walking in true purpose here on earth

I did not know how to date or just be friends
I would just turn my very being over to them

Talk about being sexually driven and just bound
There was no way by my true love I could be found

I know it will be a process and I must change what I believe
I must come out of that old mind set and know there is so much more to Queen

I must believe I am a child of the most high
There is so much more to me than what I carry between my thighs

Yes, I may be a little different and not everyone's cup of tea
What matters is I am on my way to living in that plan of abundance that God designed for me

I will no longer walk with my head hung down and in shame
I will hold my head up and walk in purpose and know Queen is not just a name

What questions and concerns do still have that were not addressed? Take your time. Be honest with yourself. Remember what you remain denial in, you cannot be healed from.

_____

_____

_____

_____

_____

_____

_____

_____

_____

_____

_____

_____

_____

_____

_____

_____

_____

_____

_____

_____

_____

_____

_____

_____

_____

_____

_____

A Word From The Author

I truly hope this workbook has been a blessing to you. My desire is to make a difference in the lives of others. If I can help one young lady not go through anything I have been through, selling her flesh and soul to someone just to think in her mind she is being loved.

You are loved!!! God loves you and so do I. Now go through your process of loving yourself.

No matter what injuries
you have suffered,
remember you are NOT
damaged goods!!!

Be Encouraged by God's Word –
Daily Reading Is Healing

Psalm 139:14

I will praise You, for I am fearfully and wonderfully made; Marvelous are Your works, And that my soul knows very well.

Romans 8:1

There is therefore now no condemnation to those who are in Christ Jesus, who do not walk according to the flesh but according to the Spirit.

Proverbs 18:21

Death and life are in the power of the tongue, And those who love it will eat its fruit.

Philippians 4:8

Finally, brethren whatever things are true, whatever things are noble, whatever things are just, whatever things are pure, whatever things are lovely, whatever things are of good report, if there is any virtue and if there is anything praiseworthy – meditate on these things

Jeremiah 29:11

For I know the thoughts that I think toward you, says the Lord, thoughts of peace and not of evil, to give you a future and a hope.

Matthew 6:33

But seek first the kingdom of God and His righteousness, and all these things shall be added to you

John 8:36

Therefore if the Son makes you free, you shall be free indeed.

*All scriptures are from the New King James Version

BIO

Author Queen Esther Lacey began her early years in the chilly region of White Plains, New York. Of the fruit of her womb yields one son and one daughter, who has yielded her two grandchildren.

While battling through childhood depression, Queen Esther wrote through her plight, after becoming inspired by a teacher who noted the gift of writing and gifted her with a book by author Langston Hughes. Through her journey of life, writing was always a part of what Queen Esther considers her "private life," until becoming the published author of her first work in 2009: "It is Not About Religion, God Wants Relationship. God's Love is Unconditional," a thoughtful depiction of personal experiences and inspirations written in poetic form. Queen Esther has since authored and published seven books to date. She has recently ventured out as a Writing Consultant for aspiring writers seeking to pen their thoughts and individual stories.

Personal Expressions by Queen, LLC. is a private line of heart touching greetings launched in 2007. Reading her artistry not only gives you a glimpse of her pain and struggles, but it shows how developing a relationship with Christ Jesus has empowered her to overcome them all! Queen Esther is one who deeply cares for the hurting and is passionate about using her gift of writing to reach multitudes of women. She ministers healing and encouragement to all who are seeking to find hope in whatever situation they find themselves.

In her free time, Queen Esther has enjoyed volunteering. She has volunteered at nursing homes, prison ministry, and the Big Brother, Big Sister programs of America.

Contact information:
(E) PEbyQueen@yahoo.com
(FB) facebook.com/QueenEstherLacey

OTHER WORKS BY THE AUTHOR

IT'S NOT ABOUT RELIGION, GOD WANTS A RELATIONSHIP
Sub-title – God's Love is Unconditional

FROM MY HEART TO YOURS
Sub-title- Nothing Shall Separate You From God's Love

SEARCHING FOR REAL LOVE?
Sub-title – It Won't be Found in Someone Else's Bed

YOUNG HEARTS NEED LOVE TOO
Sub-title – Bringing Awareness to Adults/Parents of some Struggles of the Youth

FROM THIS DAY FORWARD
Sub-title – Letting the hurts of the past die so you can live in the blessings of today

SEXUALLY DRIVEN

Sub-title – One Church Girl's Struggle with Sexual Addiction and a Desire to Be Loved

SEXUALLY DRIVEN II

Sub-title – Returning to My First Love!

Printed in the United States
by Baker & Taylor Publisher Services